Identifying The Wrights In The Goochland County, Virginia

Tithe Lists, 1732-1784

Robert N. Grant

HERITAGE BOOKS
2007

HERITAGE BOOKS
AN IMPRINT OF HERITAGE BOOKS, INC.

Books, CDs, and more—Worldwide

For our listing of thousands of titles see our website
at
www.HeritageBooks.com

Published 2007 by
HERITAGE BOOKS, INC.
Publishing Division
65 East Main Street
Westminster, Maryland 21157-5026

Copyright © 2001 Robert N. Grant

All rights reserved. No part of this book may be reproduced or transmitted in any form or by any means, electronic or mechanical, including photocopying, recording or by any information storage and retrieval system without written permission from the author, except for the inclusion of brief quotations in a review.

International Standard Book Number: 978-0-7884-1728-3

Identifying The Wrights

In The Goochland County, Virginia,

Tithe Lists

1732 to 1784

by Robert N. Grant

15 Campo Bello Court,
Menlo Park, CA 94025
650-854-0895

Revised as of October 26, 2000

© 2000, Robert N. Grant
2667A(102600)

Identifying The Wrights
In The Goochland County, Virginia,
Tithe Lists

In the Virginia State Archives are tithe lists for Goochland County, Virginia, from 1735 to 1779, listed as Accession Numbers 20930 and 24449. There are about 250 pages. The lists are not complete for each year and are sometimes just a single list. There are also duplications, as when a summary for the county was prepared based on the individual lists provided. And the list taker is not always identified.

In addition, the <u>Magazine of Virginia Genealogy</u>, Volume 33, Number 2, page 107, included a transcribed tithe list from Goochland County "Old Papers", Box 4, circa 1740-1770, but which can be dated to approximately 1732 or 1733.

Recently recovered County Court Loose Papers for Goochland County also included some tithe lists available in Goochland Titheables - Loose Papers: Tax & Fiscal Records 1747-1784, Box #T17, in the Archives Room of The Library of Virginia.

Attached is an edited list of the Wrights in those tithe lists. The information in the tithe lists has been organized by eliminating the duplicate listings where appropriate and then by identifying the various people from the patterns in the lists and other available information.

There are four separate Wright families represented in these lists and it is necessary to review the information independently known about these families before examining the lists.

<u>Family of 1730 John Wright of Goochland County</u>:

The first Wright family was that of 1730 John Wright of Goochland County. The year before the name indicates the year of death, when known, and the place after the name indicates the place of death, when known.

On September 28, 1728, by Patent Deed 14/8 John Wright acquired 333 acres of land in Goochland County on Muddy Creek on the south side of the James River.

The will of John Wright was dated on March 14, 1729/30, and probated on June 16, 1730, at Goochland County, Virginia, W.B. 1/193. The will named his wife Elizabeth and sons Meredith, William, John, and Francis, suggesting that Meredith was the oldest. In addition, 1730 John Wright directed that his widow Elizabeth would live on his son Meredith's part of his land during her widowhood, again suggesting that Meredith was the oldest son. 1730 John Wright's will also directed the sale of his land before his son Francis came of age, indicating that Francis was the youngest of the four sons. Finally, 1730 John Wright directed that land be bought for his sons and divided equally among them as they attained age 21, indicating that all had been born after March 14, 1708/9.

On November 1, 1733, at Goochland County, Virginia, D.B. 1/457 and on November 3, 1733, at Goochland County, Virginia, D.B. 1/458 Elizabeth Wright leased and sold to John Nicholls the 333 acres of land on Muddy Creek.

In July 1735 at Goochland County, Virginia, Court Order Book 3/376 Elizabeth Wright was summoned by Stephen Mallet to take administration of the estate of Merideth Wright, indicating the death of 1730 John Wright's son Meredith Wright before that date, and in August 1735 at Goochland County, Virginia, Court Order Book 3/379 Elizabeth Wright was appointed administrator of the estate of Merideth Wright. On January 20, 1735/6, at Goochland County, Virginia, W.B. 2/163 the inventory and appraisement of the estate of Meridy Wright was filed.

Family of 1779 John Wright of Prince Edward County:

The second Wright family was that of 1779 John Wright of Prince Edward County.

On June 20, 1733, by Patent Deed 15/17 a John Wright patented 300 acres of land in Goochland County on the branches of Beaverdam Creek in Goochland County. This was probably 1779 John Wright. As will be set forth below, 1779 John Wright married Anne Pryor, a daughter of John Pryor, and the land patented in P.D. 15/17 was described as adjacent to John Pryor. In addition, 1779 John Wright and Anne (Pryor) Wright later sold 700 acres of land in Goochland County on the branches of Beaverdam Creek and the land in P.D. 15/17 was on the branches of Beaverdam Creek.

On March 22, 1743, at Goochland County, Virginia, D.B. 4/340 John Wright purchased 200 acres of land on Beaverdam Creek.

The will of John Pryor dated July 24, 1755, was probated on August 19, 1755, at Goochland County, Virginia, D.B. 7/77 and named his daughter Anne Wright and grandson John Woodson.

On about May 19, 1756, at Goochland County, Virginia, Chancery Court Loose Papers, John Wright and Anne Wright filed a complaint against John Woodson for title to land given to them by Anne's father John Pryor during his lifetime. The complaint stated that John Wright and Anne (Pryor) Wright had resided on 200 acres of land held in the name of John Pryor from 1727 until John Pryor's death in 1755.

On November 14, 1757, at Goochland County, Virginia, D.B. 7/206 John Wright and Ann Wright and John Woodson sold 700 acres of land on Beaverdam Creek. Although the 700 acres sold is different from the 200 acres in dispute between Anne (Pryor) Wright and John Woodson, presumably the 200 acres was part of the 700 acres sold.

On February 6, 1764, at Prince Edward County, Virginia, D.B. 2/233 1779 John Wright purchased 420 acres of land on the north side of Plain Run and on the south side of the Appomattox River.

The will of John Wright was dated on March 18, 1775, and probated on April 20, 1779, at Prince Edward County, Virginia, W.B. 1/218 and named his wife Ann, his children David, Thomas, Obediah, Pryor, James, Elizabeth, Mary Williamson, and his grandchildren Thomas Wright, John Wright, Cloe Wright, Ann Coleman, and David Coleman. He gave his 400 acres of land in Prince Edward County to his son James.

On April 17, 1785, at Prince Edward County, Virginia, D.B. 7/163 James Wright sold his 424 acres of land on Plain Run and the Appomattox River to Pryor Wright. The legal description confirms that the same land was involved as in Deed 2/233.

In a cross-complaint dated September 13, 1819, in Files 525 and 578, Superior Court of Law and Chancery, Lynchburg, Virginia, Pryor Wright and James Wright, sons of 1779 John Wright, stated that their brother Thomas Wright had a predeceased brother John Wright and that that John Wright had a son John Wright who was a party to the suit.

No other southern Virginia Wright family yet examined had a son Obediah or a set of children including a Thomas, David, Obediah, and John Wright.

Thomas Wright, the son of 1779 John Wright of Prince Edward County, died between October 24, 1805, and December 9, 1805, at Campbell County, Virginia. His will dated on October 24, 1805, was probated on December 9, 1805, at Campbell County, Virginia, W.B. 2/226.

David Wright, the son of 1779 John Wright of Prince Edward County, died after October 1, 1790, and before June 24, 1801, probably at "the north fork of the Holston River in East Tennessee.

John Wright, the son of 1779 John Wright of Prince Edward County, must have died before the date of his father's will or before March 18, 1775, since a son John Wright was not mentioned in that will but a grandson John Wright was mentioned. That son John Wright must have been old enough to have had a son John before the signing of that will in 1775.

Obediah Wright, the son of 1779 John Wright of Prince Edward County, witnessed a deed with Charles Christian in 1757 for a transfer by William Roundtree and died on January 9, 1801, at Franklin County, Georgia.

Family of 1814 John Wright of Bedford County:

The third Wright family was that of 1814 John Wright of Bedford County.

On January 14, 1756, at Goochland County, Virginia, 1814 John Wright married Mary Pace (listed as Pierce), as set forth in The Douglas Register.

On March 17, 1757, at Goochland County, Virginia, The Douglas Register listed the birth of John Wright and Mary (Pierce/Pace) Wright's son Joseph.

On August 1, 1759, at Goochland County, Virginia, The Douglas Register listed the birth of John Wright and Mary (Pace) Wright's son John.

On March 5, 1761, at Goochland County, Virginia, The Douglas Register listed the birth of John Wright and Mary (Pierce/Pace) Wright's son James.

On August 27, 1765, at Bedford County, Virginia, D.B. 2/642 John Wright of Goochland County purchased 330 acres of land on Little Otter River from John Eckhols.

On November 14, 1765, at Goochland County, Virginia, The Douglas Register listed the birth of John Wright and Mary (Pace) Wright's daughter Ann.

On June 23, 1767, at Bedford County, Virginia, D.B. 3/111 John Wright of Goochland County recorded a new deed for the same land described in Bedford County Deed 2/642, but this time described as 300 acres and with a corrected legal description.

On January 13, 1768, at Goochland County, Virginia, The Douglas Register listed the birth of John Wright and Mary (Pace) Wright's daughter Mary.

On March 15, 1768, at Goochland County, Virginia, D.B. 9/132 Ann Pace, widow, appointed John Wright, Jr., the husband of her daughter Mary, as her attorney in fact to act for her in connection with a law suit in the General Court against Richard Stark to recover certain slaves.

No births of children for John Wright and Mary (Pace) Wright were recorded in The Douglas Register after 1768.

The Land Tax Lists for Bedford County, Virginia, listed John Wright with 330 acres of land on Little Otter from 1782 until his death in 1814.

The will of John Wright was dated on December 28, 1804, and probated on December 20, 1814, at Bedford County, Virginia, W.B. 4/146 and referred to his unnamed wife and named his children Benjamin, Joseph, Ann Watts, John, Thomas, Mary Watts, Elizabeth, and William.

The will gave his 300 acres of land to his son Benjamin Wright. The Division and Allotment of the land of 1835 Benjamin Wright of Bedford County was filed on March 27, 1837, at Bedford County, Virginia, W.B. 9/295 and the plat included with that Division and Allotment makes clear that the same land was involved as that purchased by John Wright in 1767 by Bedford County Deed 3/111.

The Pension Records for 1826 John Wright of Bedford County, a son of 1814 John Wright of Bedford County, in Virginia State Revolutionary War Pension File 463 stated that he had resided in Bedford County since 1768 and had resided previously in Goochland County.

A comparison of the children named in the will of 1814 John Wright, their dates of birth from independent evidence, and the dates of birth from The Douglas Register and the statements of 1826 John Wright in his pension file make clear that the John Wright of Goochland County who married Mary Pace in 1756 and had children in Goochland County until 1768 was the same person as 1814 John Wright of Bedford County.

Family of 1769 George Wright of Essex County:

The fourth Wright family was that of 1769 George Wright of Essex County.

On September 20, 1751, at Patent Deed 31/44 George Wright patented 1200 acres of land in Cumberland County. On November 20, 1756, at Cumberland County, Virginia, D.B. 2/309 George Wright of Essex County sold 400 acres of land in Cumberland County to George Wright, Jr. On November 20, 1756, at Cumberland County, Virginia, D.B. 2/311 George Wright of Essex County sold 400 acres of land in Cumberland County to Thomas Wright. On November 20, 1756, at Cumberland County, Virginia, D.B. 2/313 George Wright of Essex County sold 400 acres of land in Cumberland County to Ambrose Wright. On July 8, 1758, at Cumberland County, Virginia, D.B. 2/394 George Wright of Essex County sold 400 acres of land in Cumberland County to John Wright. The will of 1769 George Wright was dated September 29, 1760, probated on December 18, 1769, at Essex County, Virginia, W.B. 12/378, and gave to his sons John, George, Ambrose, and

Thomas the four hundred acres of land each of them was then living on. Although George Wright sold and bequeathed 1600 acres of land to his four sons, instead of the 1200 that he patented, this set of documents clearly identifies the George Wright of Essex County as the George Wright of Patent Deed 31/44.

Goochland County Tithe Lists:

Hening's Statutes At Large, Volume 3, page 258, included the statute of the General Assembly of Virginia passed in 1705 which defined a tithable to include all male persons over 16 years of age and all negro, mulatto, and Indian women who were not free. The list was to be compiled on June 10 of each year.

Hening's Statutes At Large, Volume 6, page 40, included the statute of the General Assembly of Virginia passed in 1748 which defined a tithable to include all male persons over 16 years of age and all negro, mulatto, and Indian women over 16 years of age, other than Indian tributaries to the Government, and all wives of free negroes, mulattos, and Indians, other than Indian tributaries to the the Government.

Identification Of Wrights In Tithe Lists:

With the background information set forth above and the information set forth in the Goochland County Tithe Lists, it is possible to identify almost all of the Wrights named in those Tithe Lists. The attached list labels each of these persons with a letter for reference in the order of their appearance in the Lists and the following will explain the identification of each of those persons.

Person A: Elizabeth (_____) Wright, Widow of 1730 John Wright of Goochland County

Person A was Elizabeth (_____) Wright, the widow of 1730 John Wright of Goochland County. Elizabeth sold her deceased husband's land in 1733, but apparently remained in the area. 1730 John Wright's will provided that Elizabeth would be allowed to live on the land of their son Meredith. Meredith died in 1735 and Elizabeth would be his heir. It follows that Elizabeth would then be listed as a separate tithable. Unfortunately, the absence of tithe lists or Wright listings for 1737 to 1745 makes it uncertain how long she remained in Goochland County.

Person B: Possibly William Wright, Son of 1730 John Wright of Goochland County

Person B was possibly William Wright, a son of 1730 John Wright of Goochland County. His appearance in the 1735 Tithe List indicates that he was born before June 11, 1719. William Wright, the son of 1730 John Wright, was born after March 14,

1708/09 and before March 14, 1729/30. If the order in which William was listed in the will of 1730 John Wright was the order of his birth, then he would have been the second of four sons and would have been born probably before 1726. However, the absence of tithe lists or Wright listings for 1737 to 1745 makes this identification uncertain.

Because of the uncertainty of this listing, this William Wright is listed again below as Person H.

Person C: 1779 John Wright of Prince Edward County

Person C was 1779 John Wright of Prince Edward County. This John Wright is identified in the various tithe lists by his son Thomas in his household in 1746 and 1748, by his slave Judy, Jude, or Judith in his household in 1746, 1748, 1752, 1754, 1755, 1756, and 1757, by his son Obediah in his household in 1752, 1754, 1755, and 1757, and by his designation as shoemaker in 1748, 1754, 1756, and 1757. The only John Wright with a son Obediah was 1779 John Wright of Prince Edward County and, similarly, the only John Wright with sons Thomas, David, and Obediah was 1779 John Wright. In addition, the listing of 1779 John Wright in the Goochland County Tithe Lists continued until 1757, indicating a move to another county after that date.

1779 John Wright of Prince Edward County purchased 420 acres of land in Prince Edward County on February 6, 1764, by Prince Edward County Deed 2/233.

The result is that 1779 John Wright of Prince Edward County was in Goochland County from 1746 to at least 1757. His first appearance in the 1746 tithe list indicates that 1779 John Wright was born before June 11, 1730. The first appearance of his son Thomas Wright in the 1746 tithe list indicates a date of birth for Thomas of before June 11, 1730. If 1779 John Wright was at least 18 years of age when his son Thomas was born, then his date of birth would be probably before 1713.

St. James Northam Parish Vestry Book 1744-1850 included a series of entries which probably related to 1779 John Wright of Prince Edward County. John Pryor was listed as keeping Ann Hooker in 1745. 1779 John Wright of Prince Edward County married Ann Pryor, the daughter of John Pryor. Thereafter, the Vestry Book included the following:

January 27, 1748: John Wright for Keeping Ann Hooker.

March 6, 1749: John Wright for keeping Anne Hooker.

October 5, 1750: John Wright for Keeping Ann Hooker.

February 6, 1752: John Wright for keeping Ann Hooker.

October 8, 1752: John Wright for Keeping Ann Hooker.

January 17, 1754: John Wright for Keeping Ann Hooker.

December 181 1754: John Wright for Keeping Ann Hooker.

October 14, 1755: John Wright for Keeping Ann Hooker.

November 9, 1756: John Wright for Keeping Ann Hooker.

November 7, 1757: John Wright for Keeping Ann Hooker.

There were no listings for John Wright keeping Ann Hooker after 1757, which is consistent with his disappearance from the Goochland tithe lists and his move to Prince Edward County in possibly 1758 and clearly by 1763.

Person D: 1805 Thomas Wright of Campbell County, Son of 1779 John Wright of Prince Edward County

Person D was 1805 Thomas Wright of Campbell County, a son of 1779 John Wright of Prince Edward County. He is identifiable in the 1746 and 1748 tithe lists in the household of John Wright the shoemaker and owner of slave Judy or Jude.

The first appearance of Thomas Wright in the John Wright household in the 1746 tithe list indicates a date of birth for Thomas Wright of before June 11, 1730.

Person E: John Wright, Son of 1779 John Wright of Prince Edward County

Person E was John Wright, a son of 1779 John Wright of Prince Edward County. He is identifiable in the 1746 tithe lists in the household of Drury Christian and in the 1747 tithe lists in the household of John Pryor. It would be appropriate for 1779 John Wright's son to be listed in the residence of a neighbor, probably as a farm hand, and to be listed in the residence of his grandfather John Pryor, probably in the same role.

The first appearance of John Wright in the Drury Christian household in 1746 indicates a date of birth for John Wright of before June 11, 1730.

The Douglas Register listed the birth on March 22, 1759, of a son Benjamin to John Wright and Judith Barns. It is not yet clear who this John and Judith (Barns) Wright couple were, but it may have been John Wright, the son of 1779 John Wright of Prince Edward County. John Wright, the son of 1779 John Wright, probably died before his father's will was written on March 18, 1775, and left a son John Wright who was party to the lawsuit filed in 1819 in Lynchburg Superior Court involving the estate of

1805 Thomas Wright of Campbell County. The dates involved would be appropriate for John Wright, son of 1779 John Wright, to have been the husband of Judith (Barns) Wright, but further research will be required to confirm that identification.

Person F: William Wright (Goochland County)

Person F was a William Wright who is designated as William Wright (Goochland County). He is identified by his appearance with one tithe in Northam Parish or the John Payne List in 1746 and 1748, by the slave Jack in his household in the 1752, 1753, 1754, 1755, 1756, 1757, 1759, 1760, 1761, 1763, 1764, 1766, and 1769 lists, and by his ownership of 100 acres of land in the 1763, 1764, 1766, and 1771 lists.

The first appearance of William Wright in 1746 as a tithe indicates a date of birth before June 11, 1730.

On March 6, 1746, at Goochland County, Virginia, D.B. 6/175 William Wright purchased 100 acres of land from John Mims, both of Goochland County. The land was sold by William Wright on January 25, 1786, at Goochland County, Virginia, D.B. 14/244. His land was adjacent to that of John Wright the carpenter, described as Person G below. In addition, in the 1771 tithe list William Wright had in his household a slave Creacy and in the 1773 tithe list Francis Wright, the son of John Wright the carpenter, listed a slave Crease. The proximity of their land with regard to the time of purchase and location and the switching of a slave between the households indicate a probable family relationship and this William Wright (Goochland County) may have been a brother of John Wright (Goochland County Carpenter).

The absence of additional tithes in the household of this William Wright throughout his time in Goochland County leaves open whether he had any male descendants, but the probability would seem to be that he did not.

Person G: John Wright (Goochland County Carpenter)

Person G was John Wright (Goochland County Carpenter). He is identifiable by the slave Jenny, Jany, or Jane in his household in 1746, 1748, 1752, 1754, 1755, by the presence of his son John Wright, Jr., in his household in 1752, 1754, 1755, and 1756, and the move of John Wright, Jr., from his household to a separate listing in 1757, and by his ownership of 120 acres of land in 1763, 1764, 1765, 1766, 1767, and 1768. He continued to be listed until 1772 in the Francis Wright household, although the writing in the 1772 tithe list was an apparently old form of "Jno" and is difficult to decipher. In the 1748 tithe list John Wright was identified as a carpenter and thus his designation above.

The initial listing of John Wright the carpenter in 1746 indicates a date of birth before June 11, 1730. The absence of his son John Wright, Jr., from the 1748 tithe list and the initial appearance of John Wright, Jr., in the 1752 tithe list indicate a date of birth for John Wright, Jr., of before June 11, 1736, and probably between June 10, 1732, and June 11, 1736. If John Wright the carpenter was at least 18 years of age at the birth of his son John Wright, Jr., his date of birth would be probably before 1719. John Wright the carpenter's son John Wright, Jr., was 1814 John Wright of Bedford County and is discussed more fully as Person M below.

On April 10, 1739, at Goochland County, Virginia, D.B. 3/213 John Wright purchased 358 acres of land on Lickinghole Creek from Robert Mimms. On September 25, 1741, at Goochland County, Virginia, D.B. 3/491 John Wright and his wife Judith sold 179 acres of that land to Stephen Clement. On November 19, 1751, at Goochland County, Virginia, D.B. 6/178 John Wright sold 60 acres of that land to Robert Pleasant. These three deeds left John Wright with 119 acres of land, or rounded 120 acres of land, the same amount as set forth in the tithe lists for John Wright the carpenter. On May 7, 1767, at Goochland County, Virginia, D.B. 9/116 John Wright mortgaged that remaining 119 acres of land and identified it as the land purchased from Robert Mimms. The result is to identify John Wright (Goochand County Carpenter) with each of the deed records listed above, to place him in Goochland County from 1739 through at least 1771, and to identify his wife as Judith (_____) Wright.

The Douglas Register listed the birth in February 1756 of a daughter Betty to John Wright and "Judah Easly on Lickinhole." Since the land of John Wright the carpenter was on Lickinghole Creek, this appears to be a clear identification of that family and his wife as Judith (Easly) Wright. In addition, the name Roderick appears in the Easley family as a son of Warham Easley and, as set forth below, John Wright the carpenter named one of his sons Roderick Wright. However, The Douglas Register also listed the birth on March 22, 1759, of a son Benjamin to John Wright and Judith Barns. It is not yet clear who this second John and Judith Wright couple were, but as set forth above, it may have been John Wright, the son of 1779 John Wright of Prince Edward County.

In 1760 John Wright the carpenter had an additional tithe of James Wright, who would be his son. The absence of James Wright from the 1759 tithe list and the initial appearance of James Wright in 1760 indicate that he was born sometime before June 11, 1744, and probably between June 10, 1743, and June 11, 1744. This James Wright is discussed as Person O below.

In 1763 John Wright the carpenter had an additional tithe of William Wright, Jr., the "Jr." indicating a younger William

Wright than Person H in the same tithe list. The absence of William Wright, Jr., from the 1761 tithe list and the initial appearance of William Wright in the tithe list in 1763 indicate a date of birth before June 11, 1747, and probably between June 10, 1745, and June 11, 1747. This William Wright is discussed as Person P below.

In 1766 John Wright the carpenter had an additional tithe of Francis Wright, another son. The absence of Francis Wright from the 1765 tithe list and the initial appearance of Francis Wright in the tithe list in 1766 indicate a date of birth before June 11, 1750, and probably between June 10, 1749, and June 11, 1750. This Francis Wright is discussed as Person Q below.

In 1769 John Wright the carpenter had an additional tithe of Rodrick Wright, another son. The absence of Roderick Wright from the 1768 tithe list and the initial appearance of Roderick Wright in the tithe list in 1769 indicate a date of birth before before June 11, 1753, and probably between June 10, 1752, and June 11, 1753. This Roderick Wright is discussed as Person R below.

<u>St. James Northam Parish Vestry Book 1744-1850</u> included the following entries which probably related to John Wright the carpenter:

October 14, 1745:

    John Wright for making Benches at the Church.

January 27, 1748:

    John Wright for taking down a pair of stairs.

May 11, 1749:

    Ordered that Tarlton Fleming, Arthur Hopkins and John Payne to view the Work done by John Wright on the Glebe House and the additional Building done by Wade Netherland.

March 6, 1749/50:

    John Wright for Horseblocks and putting putty on the windows at St. Johns Church.

September 25, 1760:

    John Wright for Work done at Upper Church.

Person H: William Wright, Son of 1730 John Wright of Goochland County

Person H was probably William Wright, a son of 1730 John Wright of Goochland County. Southam Parish (full name St. James Southam Parish) included that portion of Goochland south of the James River that became Cumberland County in 1749. The land of 1730 John Wright was on Muddy Creek on the south side of the James River. If William Wright stayed in the area near the land of his father in Goochland County after its sale in 1733, then he would appear in the Southam Parish tithe list. In addition, William Wright appeared in the Southam list along with a John Wright and, as will be set forth below, in 1748 with a Francis Wright. 1730 John Wright had sons William, John, and Francis, named in that order, probably their order of birth. The coincidence of names in the will and on the tithe lists and the coincidence of the order of their designation in the will and their appearance in the tithes lists indicates that the same people were involved.

Further records of this William Wright are found in Cumberland County after its formation in 1749. On August 28, 1749, at Cumberland County, Virginia, Court Order Book 1749-51/16 the case of William Wright versus Francis Epperson for assault and battery was continued until the next court and then confusingly, on August 28, 1749, at Cumberland County, Virginia, Court Order Book 1749-51/23 William Wright obtained a judgment against Francis Epperson for assault and battery.

On August 28, 1749, at Cumberland County, Virginia, Court Order Book 1749-51/16 the court entered a judgment against William Wright in favor of Thomas Yuille, as administrator of the estate of John Yuille, for £2 6S.

On November 27, 1749, at Cumberland County, Virginia, Court Order Book 1749-51/33 in the case of Wright v. Epperson the court granted the defendant additional time to present evidence and on March 26, 1750, at Cumberland County, Virginia, Court Order Book 1749-51/55 the court dismissed the case of Wright v. Epperson by agreement of the parties.

Finally, on June 28, 1757, at Cumberland County, Virginia, Court Order Book 1752-58/483 the court found William Wright to be a soldier and authorized the sheriff and others to find and apprehend him.

Person I: John Wright, Son of 1730 John Wright of Goochland County

Person I was probably John Wright, a son of 1730 John Wright of Goochland County. This identification is based on the same reasoning as that used for the identification of Person H, his brother William Wright.

The initial appearance of John Wright in the 1746 Tithe List indicates that he was born before June 11, 1730, but to have been named in the will of 1730 John Wright he would have had to have been born before March 14, 1729/30.

Person J: David Wright, Son of 1779 John Wright of Prince Edward County

Person J was David Wright, a son of 1779 John Wright of Prince Edward County. He appeared only once in the 1748 tithe list in the household of John Wright the shoemaker.

The absence of David Wright from the 1746 tithe list and the initial appearance of David Wright in the tithe list of 1748 indicate a date of birth before June 11, 1732, and probably between June 10, 1730, and June 11, 1732.

Person K: Francis Wright, Son of 1730 John Wright of Goochland County

Person K was probably Francis Wright, a son of 1730 John Wright of Goochland County. This identification is based on the same reasoning as that used for the identification of Persons H and I, his brothers William Wright and John Wright.

The initial appearance of Francis Wright in the 1748 tithe list indicates that he was born before June 11, 1732, but to have been named in the will of 1730 John Wright he would have had to have been born before March 14, 1729/30.

One further record of this Francis Wright is found in Cumberland County after its formation in 1749. On February 26, 1753, at Cumberland County, Virginia, Court Order Book 1752-58/59 Thomas Pleasant filed an account against Frank Wright.

Person L, 1769 George Wright of Essex County

Person L was 1769 George Wright of Essex County. As mentioned above, George Wright first purchased land in Cumberland County on September 20, 1751, by Patent Deed 31/44 and this appearance of his name in the tithe list in Southam Parish indicates that he had established a presence in the part of Goochland County which became Cumberland in 1749 and probably on the land that he patented in 1751.

Person M: 1814 John Wright of Bedford County, Son of John Wright (Goochland County Carpenter)

Person M was 1814 John Wright of Bedford County. This John Wright is identifiable in the tithe lists by his appearance in the household of John Wright the carpenter in 1752, 1754, 1755, and 1756. In 1757 John Wright, Jr., established his separate household and tithe listing, but continued to be listed as John Wright, Jr., in 1757, 1760, 1761, 1762, 1763, 1764, 1765, and 1766. John Wright, Jr., is also identifiable as owning no land in the tithe lists of 1763, 1764, 1765, 1766, 1767, and 1768. In addition, William Wright, the son of John Wright the carpenter, moved from his father's household to that of John Wright, Jr., in 1765 and then back again in 1766. John Wright, Jr., was not listed in the tithe lists after 1768.

As mentioned above, 1814 John Wright married Mary Pace in 1756 at Goochland County and the births of their children were recorded in Goochland County until early 1768, at which time they moved to Bedford County to land purchased in 1765 and 1767. The only other John Wrights in the Goochland County tithes lists through this time were John Wright the carpenter and 1779 John Wright. The coincidental timing of the marriage of 1814 John Wright of Bedford County in conjunction with the establishment of a separate household by John Wright, Jr., in the Goochland County tithe lists and the disappearance of John Wright, Jr., from the Goochland County tithe lists at the same time as the appearance of 1814 John Wright in Bedford County establishes that John Wright, Jr., the son of John Wright the carpenter, was the same person as 1814 John Wright of Bedford County.

The absence of John Wright, Jr., the son of John Wright the carpenter, from the 1748 tithe list and the initial appearance of John Wright, Jr., in the 1752 tithe list indicate that his date of birth was before June 11, 1736, and probably between June 10, 1732, and June 11, 1736.

Person N: 1801 Obediah Wright of Franklin County, Georgia, Son of 1779 John Wright of Prince Edward County

Person N was 1801 Obediah Wright of Franklin County, Georgia, a son of 1779 John Wright of Prince Edward County. Obediah Wright is identifiable in the household of 1779 John Wright of Prince Edward County in 1752, 1754, 1755, and 1757.

The absence of Obediah Wright from the 1748 tithe list and the initial appearance of Obediah Wright in the 1752 tithe list indicate a date of birth before June 11, 1736, and probably between June 10, 1732, and June 11, 1736.

Person O: James Wright, Son of John Wright (Goochland County Carpenter)

Person O was James Wright, a son of John Wright (Goochland County Carpenter). This James Wright was listed once in the 1760 tithe list in the household of John Wright the carpenter.

The absence of James Wright from the 1759 tithe list and the initial appearance of James Wright in the 1760 tithe list indicate a date of birth before June 11, 1744, and probably between June 10, 1743, and June 11, 1744.

Person P: William Wright, Son of John Wright (Goochland County Carpenter)

Person P was William Wright, a son of John Wright (Goochland County Carpenter). This William Wright is identifiable in the tithe lists as William Wright, Jr., in the household of John Wright the carpenter in 1763 and 1764, in the household of John Wright, Jr., in 1765, and back in the household of John Wright the carpenter in 1766 and 1769.

The absence of William Wright, Jr., from the 1761 tithe list and the initial appearance of William Wright, Jr., in the 1763 tithe list indicate a date of birth before June 11, 1747, and probably between June 10, 1745, and June 11, 1747.

The Douglas Register listed the marriage of William Wright and Martha Cawley on October 5, 1769, at Goochland County and the birth of their daughter Chicely on June 5, 1773, at Goochland County. As set forth below, Roderick Wright married Hannah Cawley; brothers marrying sisters was, of course, very common. Since there was only one other William Wright in the tithe lists and his indicated date of birth was before June 11, 1730, the above evidence indicates that William Wright, the son of John Wright the carpenter, was the William Wright who married Martha Cawley.

Person Q: Francis Wright, Son of John Wright (Goochland County Carpenter)

Person Q was Francis Wright, a son of John Wright (Goochland County Carpenter). Francis Wright is indentifiable in the household of John Wright (Goochland County Carpenter) in 1766 and 1767, and in his own household in 1773 with the slave Crease, who had formerly been in the household of William Wright (Goochland County), and probably with John Wright the carpenter as a member of the household. The writing for the John Wright in that tithe list was not clearly decipherable, but appears to be an old style form of "Jno".

The absence of Francis Wright from the 1765 tithe list and the initial appearance of Francis Wright in the 1766 tithe list indicate a date of birth before June 11, 1750, and probably between June 10, 1749, and June 11, 1750.

The Douglas Register listed the marriage of Francis Wright and Mercy Goldsmith on May 30, 1771, at Goochland County.

The Goochland County Court records record further litigation involving Francis Wright. In August 1772 at Goochland County, Virginia, Ct.O.B. 12/234 George Kippen & Company obtained a judgement for 8 pounds, 13 shillings, and 10 pence against Francis Wright. In May 1774 at Goochland County, Virginia, Ct.O.B. 12/245 Francis Wright recovered a judgement of 4 pounds, 19 shillings, and 11 pence against Roakes [Noakes?] McCaul. In July 1778 at Goochland County, Virginia, Ct.O.B. 13/63 Francis Wright appeared in court to answer the complaint of Prosser & Trent. In November 1778 at Goochland County, Virginia, Ct.O.B. 13/132 the case of Prosser & Trent v. Francis Wright was continued. In June 1779 at Goochland County, Virginia, Ct.O.B. 13/178 Prosser & Trent recovered a judgment of 12 pounds, 16 shillings, and 4 pence against Francis Wright. In September 1784 at Goochland County, Virginia, Ct.O.B. 15/162 the court confirmed the judgment of 12 pounds, 16 shillings, and 4 pence recovered by Prosser & Trent against Francis Wright. In March 1785 at Goochland County, Virginia, Ct.O.B. 15/221 in the case of Francis Wright v. Joseas Payne, George Payne filed a recognizance bond on behalf of Joseas Payne in the case of Francis Wright v. Joseas Payne. In May 1785 at Goochland County, Virginia, Ct.O.B. 15/290 Joseas Payne appeared to answer the complaint of Francis Wright and the case was referred to trial. On March 20, 1786, at Goochland County, Virginia, Ct.O.B. 16/29 the case of Francis Wright vs. Noakes [Roakes?] W. Caul was continued. And on August 23, 1786, at Goochland County, Virginia, Ct.O.B. 16/176 Francis Wright's suit against Josias Payne was dismissed for failure to appear.

Person R: Roderick Wright, Son of John Wright (Goochland County Carpenter)

Person R was Roderick Wright, a son of John Wright (Goochland County Carpenter). Roderick Wright is identifiable in the household of John Wright the carpenter in 1769, 1770, in his own listing in 1771, back to his father's household in 1772, and with Major Josias Payne in 1773, probably as an overseer.

The absence of Roderick Wright from the 1768 tithe list and the initial appearance of Roderick Wright in the 1769 tithe list indicate a date of birth before June 11, 1753, and probably between June 10, 1752, and June 11, 1753.

The Douglas Register listed the marriage of Roderick Wright and Hannah Cawley on October 31, 1769, at Goochland County and the births of their children Nansie on September 20, 1770, Betsey on July 3, 1773, Judith on December 16, 1774, and John on August 13, 1776.

Further records of Roderick Wright indicate his move from Goochland County. The 1782 Land Tax List for Prince Edward County, Virginia, listed Roderick Wright with 144 acres of land. The document by which this land was acquired has not as yet been located. The record indicates that Roderick Wright was possibly resident at Prince Edward County in 1782. The 1784 Land Tax List for Prince Edward County, Virginia, also listed Roderick Wright with 144 acres of land. The Personal Property Tax Lists For The Year 1787 stated that List A in Hanover County, Virginia, listed Roderick Wright in the Peter Johnson household with the following property:

Number of white males above 16 and under 21	Blacks above 16	Blacks under 16	Horses, mares, colts & mules	Cattle
0	8	11	8	32

This was probably Roderick Wright acting as an overseer for Peter Johnson. On May 23, 1792, at Goochland County, Virginia, Ct.O.B. 19/91 Adam Toler obtained a judgment for 2£, 16s, and 10p against Roderick Wright upon his failure to appear and defend.

Edited And Annotated Goochland County, Virginia, Tithe Lists

Undated Tithe List,
but probably 1732 or 1733

		Identification
Widow Wright	2	Person A, Elizabeth (_____) Wright, widow of 1730 John Wright of Goochland County

1734 Tithe List

No list yet found

1735 Tithe List

		Identification
George Taylor		
Roger Right	2	
John Cox		
William Right	1	Person B, possibly William Wright, son of 1730 John Wright of Goochland County

1736 Tithe List

		Identification
John Twitty-(between Deep Creek & Fine Creek)		
Elizabeth Right	1	Person A, Elizabeth (_____) Wright, widow of 1730 John Wright of Goochland County

1737 to 1743 Tithe Lists

No list yet found

1744 Tithe List

No Wrights listed

1745 Tithe List

No list yet found

1746 Tithe List

Northam Parish-John Smith

		Identification
William Wright	[_]	Person F, William Wright (Goochland County)
John Wright, Jenny	2	Person G, John Wright (Goochland County Carpenter)

John Payne

Jno Wright Tiths Thos Wright, Negro Judy	3	Person C, 1779 John Wright of Prince Edward County Person D, 1805 Thomas Wright of Campbell County, son of 1779 John Wright of Prince Edward County
Drury Christian, Jno Wright	2	Person E, John Wright, son of 1779 John Wright of Prince Edward County

Southam Parish-Thomas Turpin

William Wright	1	Person H, William Wright, son of 1730 John Wright of Goochland County
John Wright	1	Person I, John Wright, son of 1730 John Wright of Goochland County

1747 Tithe List

Southam Parish-Thomas Turpin

		Identification
William Wright	1	Person H, William Wright, son of 1730 John Wright of Goochland County
John Wright	1	Person I, John Wright, son of 1730 John Wright of Goochland County

1748 Tithe List

John Payne

		Identification
John Pryor, Robert Woodson, John Wright	6	Person E, John Wright, son of 1779 John Wright of Prince Edward County
John Wright Carptr Tithes Jeffry, Jany	3	Person G, John Wright (Goochland County Carpenter)
Willm. Wright List	1	Person F, William Wright (Goochland County)
Jno Wright Shoemaker Tithes Thos Wright, David Wright, Jud	4	Person C, 1779 John Wright of Prince Edward County Person D, 1805 Thomas Wright of Campbell County, son of 1779 John Wright of Prince Edward County Person J, David Wright, Sr., son of 1779 John Wright of Prince Edward County

Southam Parish

William Wright	1	Person H, William Wright, son of 1730 John Wright of Goochland County
Francis Wright	1	Person K, Francis Wright, son of 1730 John Wright of Goochland County

Charles Anderson - Southam Parish

George Wright Negs peter phellis	3	Person L, 1769 George Wright of Essex County

1749 Tithe List

    No Wrights listed

1750 Tithe List

    No list yet found

1751 Tithe List

    Thomas Starke

		Identification
William Wright, Philoman Johns Judy	3	Person F, William Wright (Goochland County)

1752 Tithe List

Thomas Starke

		Identification
[Jo]hn Wright [hi]s Son John Wright [J]enne	} 3	Person G, John Wright (Goochland County Carpenter) Person M, 1814 John Wright of Bedford County, son of John Wright (Goochland County Carpenter)
William Wright Jack	} 2	Person F, William Wright (Goochland County)

John Payne

John Wright Tythes Jude, Obadiah Wright	} 3	Person C, 1779 John Wright of Prince Edward County Person N, 1801 Obediah Wright of Franklin County, Georgia, son of 1779 John Wright of Prince Edward County

1753 Tithe List

John Smith List

		Identification
John Clement, Thomas Clement, Wm. Wright, Jack	} 4	Person F, William Wright (Goochland County)

1754 Tithe List

Thos. Stark

		Identification
John Wright John Wright Jur. Jenny	} 3	Person G, John Wright (Goochland County Carpenter) Person M, 1814 John Wright of Bedford County, son of John Wright (Goochland County Carpenter)
Wm Right Jack	} 2	Person F, William Wright (Goochland County)

George Payne

John Wright shoemaker List Obediah Wright, Negroes Jude, Jane	} 4	Person C, 1779 John Wright of Prince Edward County Person N, 1801 Obediah Wright of Franklin County, Georgia, son of 1779 John Wright of Prince Edward County

26.

1755 Tithe List

Thomas Starke

Jno Wright
    Jno Wright Jr.   } 3
    Negroe Jane

Wm. Wright list
    Wm Gilliam   } 3
    Negroe -Jack

George Payne

John Wright Tithes
    Obediah Wright   } 4
    Negros Jude Jane

Identification

Person G, John Wright (Goochland County Carpenter)
Person M, 1814 John Wright of Bedford County, son of John Wright (Goochland County Carpenter)

Person F, William Wright (Goochland County)

Person C, 1779 John Wright of Prince Edward County
Person N, 1801 Obediah Wright of Franklin County, Georgia, son of 1779 John Wright of Prince Edward County

1756 Tithe List

John Smith

		Identification
John Wright List	⎫	Person G, John Wright (Goochland County Carpenter)
John Wright jur	⎬ 3	Person M, 1814 John Wright of Bedford County, son of John Wright (Goochland County Carpenter)
Jenny	⎭	
Wm Wright Lists	⎫ 2	Person F, William Wright (Goochland County)
Negro Jack	⎭	

Will. Pryor

John Wright Shoemaker	⎫	Person C, 1779 John Wright of Prince Edward County
& his list	⎬ 2	
Negro Jude	⎭	

28.

1757 Tithe List

John Smith

		Identification
John Wright list	1	Person G, John Wright (Goochland County Carpenter)
John Wright Jun. List	1	Person M, 1814 John Wright of Bedford County, son of John Wright (Goochland County Carpenter)
William Wright List. Jack	2	Person F, William Wright (Goochland County)

William Pryor

John Wright Shoemaker & his Obediah Wright, Negro Rachael, Judith	4	Person C, 1779 John Wright of Prince Edward County Person N, 1801 Obediah Wright of Franklin County, Georgia, son of 1779 John Wright of Prince Edward County

1758 Tithe List

No list yet found

1759 Tithe List

John Smith

		Identification
John Wright List	1	Person G, John Wright (Goochland County Carpenter)
William Wright List. Jack	2	Person F, William Wright (Goochland County)

1760 Tithe List

John Smith

		Identification
John Wright, & James Wright	2	Person G, John Wright (Goochland County Carpenter) Person O, James Wright, son of John Wright (Goochland County Carpenter)
William Wright & Negroe Jack	2	Person F, William Wright (Goochland County)
John Wright Junr	1	Person M, 1814 John Wright of Bedford County, son of John Wright (Goochland County Carpenter)

1761 Tithe List

John Smith

		Identification
John Wright	1	Person G, John Wright (Goochland County Carpenter)
John Wright Jur List	1	Person M, 1814 John Wright of Bedford County, son of John Wright (Goochland County Carpenter)
William Wright & Jack	2	Person F, William Wright (Goochland County)

1762 Tithe List

Robert Page List

		Identification
John Wright	2	Person G, John Wright (Goochland County Carpenter)
John Wright junr	2	Person M, 1814 John Wright of Bedford County, son of John Wright (Goochland County Carpenter)
Will Wright	2	Person F, William Wright (Goochland County)

1763 Tithe List

William Mitchell

			Acres	Identification
John Wright Junr	Tythes 1	Land	-	Person M, 1814 John Wright of Bedford County, son of John Wright (Goochland County Carpenter)
John Wright, William Wright Jr.	Tythes 2	Land	120	Person G, John Wright (Goochland County Carpenter) Person P, William Wright, son of John Wright (Goochland County Carpenter)
William Wright, Jack	Tythes 2	Land	100	Person F, William Wright (Goochland County)

1764 Tithe List

Wil Michell

	Tythes	Land	Carages	Identification
John Wright, William Wright Junr	2	120		Person G, John Wright (Goochland County Carpenter) Person P, William Wright, son of John Wright (Goochland County Carpenter)
John Wright Junr. Robert Depriest	2	—	—	Person M, 1814 John Wright of Bedford County, son of John Wright (Goochland County Carpenter)
William Wright. Jack	2	100		Person F, William Wright (Goochland County)

1765 Tithe List

	Tythes	Land	Carages	Identification
John Wright	1	120		Person G, John Wright (Goochland County Carpenter)
John Wright Junr William Wright Junr	2	—		Person M, 1814 John Wright of Bedford County, son of John Wright (Goochland County Carpenter) Person P, William Wright, son of John Wright (Goochland County Carpenter)

1766 Tithe List

	Tythes	Land	Carages	Identification
William Wright, Jack	2	100		Person F, William Wright (Goochland County)
John Wright Junr. James	2			Person M, 1814 John Wright of Bedford County, son of John Wright (Goochland County Carpenter)
John Wright, William Wright, Francis Wright	3	120		Person G, John Wright (Goochland County Carpenter) Person P, William Wright, son of John Wright (Goochland County Carpenter) Person Q, Francis Wright, son of John Wright (Goochland County Carpenter)

1767 Tithe List

John Smith

		Identification
John Wrights list Negro Jams, francis Wright, 120 acres land	} 3	Person G, John Wright (Goochland County Carpenter) Person Q, Francis Wright, son of John Wright (Goochland County Carpenter)
John Wright Junr list	1	Person M, 1814 John Wright of Bedford County, son of John Wright (Goochland County Carpenter)
William Wrights list Negro Jack 100 acres land	} 2	Person F, William Wright (Goochland County)

1768 Tithe List

William Harrison

Persons Names who are Chargeable	Names of the Tithables	No. of Tithes	No. Cariage	Quan of Land	Identification
Wright John		1			Person M, 1814 John Wright of Bedford County, son of John Wright (Goochland County Carpenter)
Wright John Senr	Dick	2		120	Person G, John Wright (Goochland County Carpenter)

1769 Tithe List

William Harrison

			Identification
William Wright, Jack	}	2	Person F, William Wright (Goochland County)
John Wright list William Wright Rodrick Wright	}	3	Person G, John Wright (Goochland County Carpenter) Person P, William Wright, son of John Wright (Goochland County Carpenter) Person R, Roderick Wright, son of John Wright (Goochland County Carpenter)

36.

1770 Tithe List

Stephen Simpson

		Identification
John Wright	3 ⎫	Person G, John Wright (Goochland County Carpenter)
Rhederick Wright	2 ⎭	Person R, Roderick Wright, son of John Wright (Goochland County Carpenter)

Jesse Payne

		Identification
Wm Right list Wm Ryan	2	Person F, William Wright (Goochland County)

1771 Tithe List

	Tythes	Land	No. Carages	Identification
Rodrick Wright List John Ryan	2			Person R, Roderick Wright, son of John Wright (Goochland County Carpenter)
John Wright List	1			Person G, John Wright (Goochland County Carpenter)
William Wright List William Ryan, Creacy	3 ⎫ ⎭	100		Person F, William Wright (Goochland County)

37.

1772 Tithe List

Wil: Michell

		Identification
William Wright List	1	Person F, William Wright (Goochland County)
John Wright List, Roderick Wright	2	Person G, John Wright (Goochland County Carpenter) Person R, Roderick Wright, son of John Wright (Goochland County Carpenter)

1773 Tithe List

		Identification
Majr Josias Payne List Rodorick Wright York, peter, Tom, Tom, Tom, Sam Squire, Diner, Jane, Mole	12	Person R, Roderick Wright, son of John Wright (Goochland County Carpenter)
Francis Wright List. Crease, [Jno?] Wright	3	Person Q, Francis Wright, son of John Wright (Goochland County Carpenter) Person G, John Wright (Goochland County Carpenter)
William Wright Junr List	1	Person F, William Wright (Goochland County) or Person P, William Wright, son of John Wright (Goochland County Carpenter)

38.

1774 Tithe List

Thomas Underwood List - St. James Northam Parish

		Identification
Thos Payne, Francis Wright Patrick Mageth, Nell London Jamey Moll. Sue Nice for Jos. Payne Jr	10	Person Q, Francis Wright, son of John Wright (Goochland County Carpenter)

1775 Tithe List

David Ross List

		Identification
Francis Wright	1	Person Q, Francis Wright, son of John Wright (Goochland County Carpenter)

1776 Tithe List

No Wrights listed

1777 Tithe List

No Wrights listed

1778 Tithe List

   No Wrights listed

1779 Tithe List

   No Wrights listed

1780 Tithe List

   No Wrights listed

1781 Tithe List

   No list yet found

1782 Tithe List

   No Wrights listed

1783 Tithe List

No list yet found

1784 Tithe List

No Wrights listed

I wish to express my appreciation to Loretta June Wright who noted and pointed out to me some of the information relating to 1779 John Wright of Prince Edward County and his children and the Pryor family that I had not noticed, to William L. Hopkins who proofed and corrected my copies of the tithe listings for Wrights, and to John S. Hopewell who graciously assisted me with the Goochland County loose papers which he is organizing.

INDEX

Barns, Judith, 9, 11
Cawley, Hannah, 16, 18
Cawley, Martha, 16
Christian, Charles, 5
Christian, Drury, 9, 21
Clement, John, 25
Clement, Stephen, 11
Clement, Thomas, 25
Coleman, Ann, 4
Cox, John, 19
Creacy, 10, 37
Crease, 10, 16, 38
David, Coleman, 4
Depreist, Robert, 33
Diner, 38
Easley, Roderick, 11
Easley, Warham, 11
Easly, Judah, 11
Eckhols, John, 5
Epperson, Frances, 13
Fleming, Tarlton, 12
Gilliam, William, 27
Goldsmith, Mercy, 17
Harrison, William, 36
Hooker, Ann, 8, 9
Hopkins, Arthur, 12
Jack, 10, 25, 26, 27, 28, 30, 31, 32, 33, 34, 35, 36
James, 34
Jamey, 39
Jams, 35
Jane, 10, 26, 27, 38
Jany, 10, 23
Jeffry, 23
Jenne, 25
Jenny, 10, 21, 26, 28
Johns, Philoman, 24
Johnson, Peter, 18
Jud, 23
Jude, 8, 9, 25, 26, 27, 28
Judith, 8, 29
Judy, 8, 9, 21, 24
Kippen, George, 17
London, 39
Mageth, Patrick, 39
Mallet, Stephen, 3
McCaul, Noakes [Roakes?], 17
McCaul, Roakes [Noakes?], 17

Mimms, Robert, 11
Mitchell, William, 32, 33, 38
Mole, 38
Moll, 39
Nell, 39
Netherland, Wade, 12
Nice, 39
Nicholls, John, 3
Pace, Ann, 5
Pace, Mary, 5, 15
Page, Robert, 31
Payne, George, 17, 26, 27
Payne, Jesse, 37
Payne, John, 10, 12, 20, 25
Payne, Jos, 39
Payne, Joseas, 17
Payne, Josias, 17, 38
Payne, Thomas, 39
Peter, 23, 38
Phellis, 23
Pleasant, Robert, 11
Pleasant, Thomas, 14
Prosser & Trent, 17
Pryor, Anne, 3, 8
Pryor, John, 3, 8, 9, 23
Pryor, William, 28, 29
Rachel, 29
Right, Roger, 19
Right, William, 19, 37
Ross, David, 39
Ryan, John, 37
Ryan, William, 37
Sam, 38
Simpson, Stephen, 37
Smith, John, 25, 28, 29, 30, 31, 35
Squire, 38
Starke, Thomas, 24, 25, 26, 27
Sue, 39
Taylor, George, 19
Toler, Adam, 18
Tom, 38
Turpin, Thomas, 22
Underwood, Thomas, 39
Watts, Ann, 6
Watts, Mary, 6
William, Roundtree, 5
Williamson, Mary, 4

Woodson, John, 3, 4
Woodson, Robert, 23
Wright, Ambrose, 6
Wright, Ann, 4, 5
Wright, Anne, 3, 4
Wright, Anne (Pryor), 3, 4
Wright, Benjamin, 6, 9, 11
Wright, Betsey, 18
Wright, Betty, 11
Wright, Chicely, 16
Wright, Cloe, 4
Wright, David, 4, 8, 14, 23
Wright, Elizabeth, 2, 3, 4, 6, 7, 19
Wright, Francis, 2, 3, 10, 12, 13, 14, 16, 17, 23, 34, 35, 38, 39
Wright, George, 6, 7, 14, 23
Wright, James, 4, 5, 11, 16, 30
Wright, John, 2, 3, 4, 5, 6, 7, 8, 9, 10, 11, 12, 13, 14, 15, 16, 17, 18, 19, 20, 21, 22, 23, 25, 26, 27, 28, 29, 30, 31, 32, 33, 34, 35, 36, 37, 38, 39
Wright, Joseph, 6
Wright, Judith, 18
Wright, Judith, 11
Wright, Judith (Barns), 9, 10
Wright, Judith (Easly), 11
Wright, Mary, 5
Wright, Mary (Pace), 5
Wright, Meredith, 2, 3, 7
Wright, Meridy, 3
Wright, Nansie, 18
Wright, Obadiah, 25
Wright, Obediah, 4, 5, 8, 15, 25, 26, 27, 29
Wright, Pryor, 4
Wright, Rhedorick, 37
Wright, Roderick, 11, 12, 16, 17, 18, 36, 37, 38
Wright, Rodorick, 38
Wright, Rodrick, 12, 36, 37
Wright, Thomas, 4, 7, 8, 9, 10, 21, 23

Wright, William, 2, 6, 7, 8, 10, 11, 12, 13, 14, 15, 16, 19, 20, 21, 22, 23, 24, 25, 26, 27, 28, 29, 30, 31, 32, 33, 34, 35, 36, 37, 38
York, 38
Yuille, John, 13
Yuille, Thomas, 13

OTHER BOOKS BY THE AUTHOR

Wright Family Personal Property Tax Records for Bedford County, Virginia, 1782 to 1850
Wright Family Records: Births in Bedford County, Virginia
Wright Family Census Records, Bedford County, Virginia, 1810-1900
Wright Family Records, Land Tax List, Bedford County, Virginia, 1782-1850
Wright Family Birth Records, (1853-1896) and Marriage Records (1788-1915): Franklin County, Virginia, 1853-1896
Wright Family Census Records, Franklin County, Virginia, 1810-1900
Wright Family Land Grants 1785-1900 And Deed Records 1785-1897, Franklin County, Virginia
Wright Family Land Tax Lists: Franklin County, Virginia, 1786-1860
Wright Family Personal Property Tax Lists: Franklin County, Virginia, 1786-1850
The Identification of 1809 William Wright of Franklin County, Virginia, as the Son of 1792 John Wright of Fauquier County, Virginia and Elizabeth (Bronaugh) (Darnall) Wright
Wright Family Death Records, 1854-1920, Cemetery Records by Cemetery, and Probate Records, 1785-1928, Franklin County, Virginia
Wright Family Birth Records, 1853 to 1896, and Marriage Records, 1782 to 1900, Campbell County, Virginia
Wright Family Personal Property Tax List Campbell County, Virginia 1785-1850
Wright Family Death Records (1853-1920), Cemetery Records By Cemetery, And Probate Records (1782-1900), Campbell County, Virginia
Wright Family Census Records Campbell County, Virginia 1810-1900
Wright Family Records: Prince Edward County, Virginia: Birth Records, Marriage Records, Election Polls, and Tithe List, Personal Property Tax List, Census
Wright Family Land Records, Bedford County, Virginia
Wright Family Records: Marriages in Bedford County, Virginia
Wright Family Deed Records 1782-1900 and Land Tax List 1782-1850, Campbell County, Virginia
Wright Family Records Lynchburg, Virginia, Birth Records 1853-1896, Marriage Records 1805-1900, Marriage Notices 1794-1880, Census Records 1900, Deed Records 1805-1900, Death Records 1853-1896, Probate Records 1805-1900
Wright Family Records: Prince Edward County, Virginia, Land Grants, Deed Records, Land Tax List, Death Records, Probate Records
Wright Family Records: Appomattox County, Virginia, Birth Records, Marriage Records, and Personal Property Tax Lists
Wright Family Records: Appomattox County, Virginia, Census Records, Deed Records, Land Tax Lists, Death Records, Probate Records

www.ingramcontent.com/pod-product-compliance
Lightning Source LLC
Chambersburg PA
CBHW081502040426
42446CB00016B/3364